Beppe Cooks!

RECIPES FROM THE HOMELAND

By Italian Guitarist Beppe Gambetta

Beppe Gambetta ♫

PHOTOGRAPHS BY RICK GARDNER
EDITED BY MARY GARDNER
DESIGNED BY MATTHEW DAVIS & JERRY HERRING

PUBLISHED BY HERRING PRESS

1996

Beppe Cooks!
Published by
Herring Press
1216 Hawthorne
Houston, Texas 77006
(713) 526-1250
e-mail: jherring@herringdesign.com

©1996 Herring Press
Text ©1996 Beppe Gambetta
Photography ©1996 Rick Gardner

Additional photography:
Pages 4 and 7
©1996 Stefano Goldberg
Pages 43 and 44–45
©1996 Hans-Bernd Sick

Written by Beppe Gambetta
Edited by Mary Gardner
Principal photography by Rick Gardner
Designed by Matthew Davis and Jerry Herring
Production coordination by Laura Dignazio
Printed by Sung In Printing/Korea

ISBN 0-917001-12-5
Library of Congress 96-76789

Distributed by
MG & Associates
P.O. Box 25042
Houston, Texas 77265
(713) 665-8228

❧ *Recipes From the Homeland* ❧

Beppe with Maria at Trattoria da Maria
in the historic center of Genoa

How does that old joke go? In heaven the chefs will be French... in hell the chefs will be English...and so on. Notice that Italian chefs don't fit either place. That's because Italian cooking is so good, it must be wicked and sinful. Because it doesn't fit any of those afterlife destinations, real Italian food is one of the two things that make it worthwhile to live a long time in this life. The other, of course, is guitar music.

In your hand you hold a book that is, miraculously, about both things that make life beautiful: Italian cooking and guitar music. It has been my very great privilege to be on the road playing concerts many times with the author of this book; he is one of the best players in the current worldwide golden age of the guitar. And he is the best damned pasta cook who ever picked the "Wildwood Flower."

So, read on, my friends, and enjoy a very Italian and inspired combination of two of life's greatest gifts. This book invites you to listen to those melodies of Italian food and chew on those flavors of the steel string guitars. And vice versa. And don't worry—if you spill the sauce on your instrument, a little dab of Chianti will set it permanently, and you can tell the story for years.

Dan Crary

Acknowledgements

This book is primarily inspired by the recipes of Mamma Gambetta and Zia Maria, who transmitted to me all the family recipes and a love for good cooking. Other people provided suggestions, recipes and help, and for this I thank Luigi Grechi, Paolo De Bernardin, Mafalda Santamaria, Roberto Franzoni, Filippo Gambetta, Stephanie Ledgin and Paolo Argenziano. The photographs from Europe were made by Stefano Goldberg and Hans-Bernd Sick (who also gently pushed me into the food world by organizing my first cooking workshop). A big help was given with ideas and the first rough draft of recipes and topics by Sandra Sarti. Special thanks to guitarist and professor Dan Crary, not only for the nice preface but also for his constant support of this project, my cooking and my music.

In Houston, my work was assisted in many ways by Susan Roeth, Mary Conn, Alessadra Leto McGhee, Leslie Frasier, Nancy Davis, Maria Camillo, Juliet Emery, James Scoggan, Greg and Mary Ann Harbar and the insuperable radio station KPFT. Special thanks to Williams–Sonoma.

Thanks to Jerry Herring, Laura Dignazio and Matt Davis of Herring Design for being so creatively involved and for understanding so well the spirit of this book.

The biggest acknowledgement for this book goes to Rick and Mary Gardner, whose philanthropic and artistic sense is recognized by hundreds of artists in Houston and throughout the whole country. Rick and Mary not only created the great food and music photographs but literally invented and sponsored the book in every little step, from the first experimental photograph of pesto to the final release party after which everyone smelled of garlic.

NOTE: We decided to leave some of my typical English mistakes in the book to give you the impression of a person from far away visiting and talking to you in your kitchen. Also, every recipe will include not only a suggested wine to accompany the food but also what music to enjoy during the meal. The choice will be not the "Top Forty" but music that I especially love. I will generally suggest three selections per meal: one Italian classic, one Italian various or ethnic and one of music that I particularly like from other parts of the world.

One other important consideration is that this book comes from a basic "let's have fun" purpose. You hear so many food photography stories about food sprayed with varnish or faked or not cooked to have a better color. We didn't do it this way and for a very good reason. All the food in this adventure was eaten with pleasure, and we had also some big "leftover" parties with musicians and friends at the end of some cooking and photo sessions.

❧ *A Few Words From Beppe* ❧

"Beppe Cooks!" isn't the usual cookbook. You will understand from the first look that it is not written by a "real" cook but by a musician on the road. This unprofessional status brings many advantages—first of all, the experience. The musician's life brings me so many times to the house of a friend who asks me at the last minute to cook with only a few ingredients, and in a short time, a good Italian meal for eleven people.

After many years of experience, I know a lot about foreign kitchens. I can find ingredients and tools in every remote, unknown cupboard or improvise at the last minute a mechanical colander with a special positioned lid. A bottle can become a rolling pin. A pizza slicer can become a ravioli cutter. Usually some friend will help to cut the onions and someone else will fly out to buy the missing ingredients (American grocery store—what a great invention!). In a corner will start the first little jam session and soon the first bottle of wine will be open. Sometimes you don't know exactly why, but the company, the food and the music will create a magic, unrepeatable moment that you will remember for the whole of your life.

Beppe in kitchen of Trattoria da Maria

Often the meal is the only moment when all the family or the friends are united to share a custom that is as long-standing as the world. Eating should not be only nourishing but also a rite that cultivates the spirit and mind—like music. In my opinion, "essere una buona forchetta," to be a hearty eater, doesn't mean to be like a well without a bottom or to eat every kind of food without end. It means to have good taste in choice and to enjoy the well-prepared cooking.

I like plain and wholesome food. I also enjoy the traditional dishes of every place I have visited and appreciate the value of the cultural meaning of cooking. For this reason, I attempt to write this book and give you the possibility to discover some new recipe that has done something special for me and has fashioned a particular moment of my life. In this way, you can understand how important it is for me to be able to prepare and enjoy a meal with friends while listening to some good music and being exposed to good vibrations.

Buon Appetito,

Beppe ♪♫

IMPROVISATION

We find improvisation in both music and cooking. It is a process that raises the natural instinct of every good cook and talented musician. Generally, the fun of the improvisation is not only the taste of the great food that is produced but also the challenge of assembling the few ingredients that the improviser can find in the house. A big part of the fun can also be the conditions that bring the improvised meal—some unexpected good friends knocking at the door, an unexpected attack of hungriness, maybe in the deep of the night after some passionate love moments or, more normally and usually, after driving home from a gig.

The improv should be short and if you have some "basics" in your house, the improv will be easy. Here are some examples of quick food prepared with nearly nothing in the house:

pasta with oil, garlic and red pepper
pasta with oil, garlic and romano cheese
pasta with butter and sage
   or with butter and nutmeg
pasta with gorgonzola
pasta with tomatoes, basil and oil
pasta with mozzarella, tomatoes and oil
bruschetta with tomatoes
bruschetta with melted cheese

In this improvising process it is really important to know about some basic food affinities and about ingredients that bring the tastes together. In the pasta, Parmesan and pecorino are the best "bring-together" ingredients but also some spoons of cream, egg yolk or a sprinkle of parsley can do a great job.

THE ART OF COOKING BY EYE OR SENSE

If we like to make the parallel with the musical world, this art is comparable to the art of playing by ear. It is the art to understand with a look the right amount of ingredients you need without weighing them precisely and to change them or improvise if necessary—in Italian "cucinare ad occhio," in English by "eye or sense."

People develop these "chops" with long experience. Often, "nonne" (grandmas) are the best cooks by sense, and in my personal experience Nonna Gambetta, Nonna Palma and Nonna Oma were the best at this art and some of the good feelings of this book comes from them.

Also, many housewives or househusbands with experience are able to prepare good dishes without weighing any ingredients. This means that every time the food will have a little surprise. The positive aspect of this way of working is that every time the food can be adjusted to the taste that the situation requires. Old relative with bad teeth will be your guest? The food will become more soft. Children will be your guest? The food will be less spicy and more sweet. One ingredient isn't tasty enough? You will add some more. One ingredient is missing? You will find the right substitute. One ingredient is particularly good? You will take care to leave this taste more "in front." Banjo player will be your guest? Just open a box of macaroni and cheese. (This dish is also recommended for viola players, drummers, and accordion players.)

Of course, this way of cooking is not obligatory, but it's fun and it's a first step to start to invent food.

NECESSARY INSTRUMENTS OF THE KITCHEN

mezzaluna
half–moon mincing knife

tagliere
cutting board

mortaio
marble mortar

pestello
wooden pestle

asse da impastare
large board for rolling out pasta

mattarello
rolling pin

stampi per cuocere
baking sheets

padella
skillet, several sizes

casseruola
saucepan, several sizes

teglia
baking pan, several sizes

cheese grater
fine

pressa per aglio
garlic press

pepper grinder

zucchini grater
small julienne

large mixing bowls

wooden spoon set

set of quality knives

large pots for cooking pasta

scolapasta grande
large colander

pasta fork

large, shallow bowls for serving pasta

large serving platters

Terra–cotta pots *seem to be sometimes magic. Food seems to enjoy a lot to be cooked in them, especially soups, stews and slow simmering sauces. Sometimes the results are so good that you cannot explain why.*

For most cooking, **cast iron kitchenware** *can be better than the terra–cotta because in cast iron you don't find any glazing and therefore any lead. Furthermore, they are unbreakable and nearly anti–adhesive if you first prepare them with a little oil.*

Sometimes the chef becomes attached to his fine tools like the musician to his instruments. I can understand this really well because when I am in my kitchen with my great family tools, I can work so much better. Fine cookware is like the instrument. The better the instrument, the easier it is for you to express your art, and the more you use it, the more it keeps a good energy.

INGREDIENTS

I would like to suggest what is useful to always have in supply. As soon as you use an item, replace it so you will never be without it. In this way, you can cope with every sort of situation or event.

pasta
a variety of shapes

rice
Italian Arborio

white flour

corn meal

sugar

salt
fine ground

salt
coarse Mediterranean sea salt

black peppercorns

dried spices

dried porcini mushrooms

vinegar
wine, herb, balsamic

extra virgin olive oil

capers in salt

green and black olives

bouillon cubes

anchovies in salt or oil

whole dried red peppers

cayenne pepper

pinenuts

raisins

canned peeled tomatoes

tomato paste

coffee

bittersweet cocoa

bread crumbs

jams and marmalades

dried beans

dried lentils

frozen peas

cookies

  amaretti
  Italian macaroons

  savoiardi
  ladyfingers

gelato
ice cream

sorbetto
sorbet, especially lemon

INGREDIENTS

PERISHABLE FOOD TO KEEP IN SUPPLY:

potatoes	**fruits**	**milk**
onions	**parsley**	**cream**
a string of garlic	**tomatoes**	**breads**
carrots	**eggs**	**variety of cheeses**
celery	**butter**	**pancetta**
lemons	**margarine**	*Italian bacon*

FROZEN FOOD TO KEEP IN SUPPLY:

I don't like the taste of frozen food a lot, so my freezer contains only some frozen focaccia, bread, fish and meat for last moment emergencies. I try to buy most ingredients fresh just before preparing the meal. Probably this is a food utopia, but I continue to dream and hope for a world with less hurry and more time to buy and enjoy food with friends and music.

the herb garden

A little garden of aromatic herbs (marjoram, sage, rosemary, thyme, etc.) and a big vase of basil always ready could make you and your meals a lot more happy. It brings great satisfaction to use your home-grown herbs. It puts you in contact with nature even if you don't have the space or time to have a real vegetable garden.

the wine cellar

Special care should be taken to include some of the Italian wines that I have suggested in the recipes. Some wines will be enjoyed during the meal and other wines (especially the whites) will be used in cooking. Your cellar should contain also Marsala to drink or to prepare sweets like Tiramisù or Zabaione, Moscato and Vin Santo to accompany the sweets, Prosecco and other sparkling wines for aperitivo and other nice moments and some liquors such as Martini, Campari and particularly Grappa for the digestion.

parmigiano–reggiano

Although you will see many "brands" of Parmesan, Parmigiano–Reggiano is the real thing. It is an artisan-made cheese, aged 18 months to 3 years, and comes in large wheels with "Parmigiano–Reggiano"

stenciled repeatedly on the golden-colored rind. It is available in most quality groceries and specialty cooking shops. But also Grana Padano is a good quality cheese to grate and sometimes it costs a little less. Wrapped tightly with plastic, Parmesan will keep in the refrigerator for up to 3 months, so you can buy a large piece to freshly grate as you need it. (Do not throw away the rind. Wrap it and store it in the freezer to use in making soups.)

pecorino *(often in the US it is called romano)*

Pecorino is a cheese made from sheep's milk and gets its name from "pecora," the Italian word for sheep. It can be eaten fresh as table cheese or more often, if aged, it can be used in the same way as Parmesan. Pecorino has a stronger flavor, more of a "bite," than Parmesan and can enhance the flavor of more spicy dishes. In Italy you can commonly find pecorino romano from the region of Rome and pecorino sardo from the island of Sardinia. I personally prefer the taste of sardo. I find it a little less salty. If you find it, you should try it and let me know what you think.

olive oil

Use only extra virgin olive oil from some Mediterranean area. The name extra virgin is

INGREDIENTS

important, especially if imported from Italy, because by Italian law it is a warranty of good quality. First cold pressed is even better but really expensive. Olive oils vary in color and taste depending on the olive used and where the oil is made. Now that they are found so easily, even in supermarkets, you can try different ones and choose your favorite. It could be good to use gentle, fine-tasting oil for plain dishes and cloudy, strong-tasting oil for more spicy dishes. You should learn to concentrate on the flavor of the oil by tasting it just on a little piece of bread.

balsamic vinegar

Balsamic vinegar comes from Modena in northern Italy and is made from sweet white Trebbiano grapes. It has a deep brown color and a sour–sweet taste unlike any other wine vinegar. Although artisan-made balsamic vinegar may be hard to find and very expensive, there are commercial balsamic vinegars from Modena available in many quality supermarkets. Balsamic vinegar can be used in marinades, sprinkled on dishes like Buttero's Chicken or paired with olive oil to bring out a special freshness to any salad.

porcini mushrooms

Mushrooms are a very important ingredient of the Italian cuisine, and every gourmet cook knows how to recognize and use many different kinds of them. Ovuli are great in a salad, colombine will make a stew fantastic, galletti are perfect preserved in oil, but the king of the mushroom is the porcini. They grow in our mountains during the period from April to November and usually peak around the end of August and beginning of September. In that period our mountains are invaded by hordes of porcini searchers and the spirit of the Gold Rush revives in our woods.

Porcini are extremely versatile. They are used fresh or dry, usually more in front if fresh and more as a bottom for the taste if dry. If you find them fresh, you can also freeze them and incredibly they won't lose their great fragrancy. If you buy them dried, check the smell, condition (better if not broken) and the expiration date. Before you use them, soak and wash them in water. This water is precious, so strain it and use it in cooking.

prosciutto *(ham)*

Prosciutto can be crudo, raw (cured), or cotto, cooked. Prosciutto crudo is the most precious and inimitable. It can be used in appetizers and sandwiches or cooked to give great flavor to pasta sauces, soups or second courses. The better way to eat it is to put its taste in front, accompanying it with just wine, bread or cantaloupe.

Prosciutto crudo is produced all over Italy with different "religious" procedures that go back in history to Roman times and that change in every region. San Daniele and Parma are the two most famous prosciutti but I personally like also the prosciutto Toscano. It is less refined but with great taste and character, like some music that I love. To enhance the flavor, prosciutto needs to be sliced as thin as possible. A good idea is to ask for a little taste before buying it.

pancetta *(bacon)*

Pancetta is the same cut of the pork as bacon but it is cured differently than American bacon. Generally it is cured under salt or pepper and sometimes smoked with different procedures in different regions. You can find it flat or rolled up in a salami shape. Good quality pancetta is often eaten raw like prosciutto, but the most important role of this ingredient is to be sautéed to flavor many Italian dishes.

THE BASIC SECRETS

Every good cook has his own secrets and some of these secrets are impossible to get. Even if you follow him the whole time in every corner of the kitchen, he will find the way to cheat you and hide the secret. In this case, the methods to convince him are really complicated or non-existing. You could try to bring him to total drunkenness and stay sober yourself. Or marry his favorite daughter. Or, if you are a spy, install a microcamera in the area of the cooker. But I don't warranty any success.

In the reality, it's not necessary to know every secret of the high cuisine, and in some cases even I joke with friends by telling them "tricks" or "secrets" that are really normal, basic rules of good cuisine that everyone should know. Here, I will point out some of the most important:

1) *Pasta needs to boil in a really big pot: if possible, 4–5 quarts of water for 1 pound of pasta. Cook at a lively but not too fierce a boil until it is "al dente."*

2) *Salt goes into the boiling water just before adding pasta. The better salt is coarsely ground sea salt.*

3) *To drain the pasta requires a special technique. Some little amount of water needs to stay with the pasta to give better consistency, so you don't have to drain it totally. Throw the pasta from the colander into the serving bowl when the water is still dripping. You have to make the decision related to the desired liquidity of the sauce. The moment when it is dripping slowly is the best.*

4) *The work of peeling fresh tomatoes will be easier if you first put them in some boiling water for a few seconds. Let them cool a little and take away the skins.*

5) *To remove the skins from fresh garlic, place one clove under the flat blade of a wide chef's knife and strike the knife just hard enough to loosen the skin. This will save you lots of time.*

6) *For mincing ingredients like fresh herbs or garlic, use a half-moon "mezzaluna," (curved blade with a handle at both ends). Not only is it fast and easy, but mincing in this way maintains the fresh flavor of the ingredients better than using an electric processor.*

7) *Use the right plates. You will eat pasta in a more enjoyable way in a large, shallow bowl-shaped plate. The pasta will stay warm until the end and be easier to get on the fork.*

❧ *Before & After* ❧

When I have foreign guests, I always try to walk with them down the flight of my stairs around twenty past noon to let them directly smell the importance of food in the Italian lifestyle. Food and the rituals connected with it are a strong part of every Italian social mechanism – like music in Ireland, tea in England or flowers in Hawaii. Because of this, people leave my country with a strong sense of all the moments that lead to the meal and all those that bring the meal to its end. To have the complete Italian experience, you should try sometime to lose yourself in the world of aperitifs, appetizers and digestives, "aperitivo, antipasto and digestivo."

Aperitivo is generally a cocktail or a sparkling wine that people drink with some little hors d'oeuvre and conversation. The most famous Italian aperitivo is called "Negroni." You prepare it in a glass of ice with ⅓ of Campari, ⅓ Martini Rosso, ⅓ of gin, and a slice of orange on the edge of the glass. Much more common is to drink a glass of good sparkling Italian wine like Prosecco. Another apertivo is less expensive white wine "corrected" with some Bitter, Vermouth or sparkling water. This cheap invention has different regional names, "Biancamaro," "Spritz," etc. What makes this aperitivo experience special is the atmosphere, the company and the conversation you will have in the bar during and after drinking. If you are ever traveling to Italy, even if you don't speak the same language you will communicate perfectly because Italians will try their best with hand language, smiles, mimics and a few words from Beatles songs. Remember to say "salute!" or "cin cin!" when the glasses hit together for a toast.

Antipasto are appetizers (*see* TWINS, ROASTED PEPPERS *and* BRUSCHETTA) and in some restaurants or some special occasions, like weddings, can be so good and numerous they kill any possibility to eat more food.

At the end of the meal (after the cheese course, the fruit course and the sweets) is finally the right moment for espresso coffee and a little digestive drop of Grappa. The taste of Grappa (liquor from distilled grapes) can be difficult to understand if not related with the end of the meal. The best way to enjoy Grappa is to chill it and sip it immediately after espresso or, better, in the espresso (caffé corretto) like 90 percent of Italians in northeast regions are doing.

Sorbetto al Limone is in my opinion the king of digestives. Sorbetto is the perfect end to every great "eatalian" meal. In Italy, quality lemon sorbetto is handmade by artisans in their shops. The color is white with some bits of lemon and even an occasional seed. To serve sorbetto as shown in the photograph of CASTAGNACCIO, mix lemon sorbet with vodka or a quality sparkling wine until it becomes liquid enough to drink through a straw.

After the digestives following dinner is a great moment to start a jam session. If after lunch, it could be better to take a nap. See my suggestions at page 61.

The Recipes!

FROM THE HOMELAND

It is probably inappropriate to call the Twins "recipes" because to prepare them you simply arrange two ingredients on a plate and that's it! However, eaten together the flavor of these combinations is phenomenal. It has the intensity of a musical duet. The Twins are used usually as appetizers, but some of them are also perfect as desserts or used as a second course. Adjust the amount of ingredients depending on the number of guests and how you serve the Twins. To understand the philosophy of these food combinations, you can think of the combinations you commonly find at American parties—celery and cheese, carrots and Béarnaise, cauliflower and blue cheese, chips and salsa, etc. Here are a few of the most common Italian combinations plus a couple of unusual exotic ones.

FICHI E SALAME

{ fresh figs and salami }

The most delicious autumn dish that you can prepare. I suggest green figs but also dark figs are really great if they are really ripe.

Arrange sliced salami and figs in a pleasant way on a serving dish.

INGREDIENTS:
½ **pound of Italian salami**   **2 pounds of fresh figs**
SUGGESTED WINES: **Rossese from Dolceacqua**
RECOMMENDED LISTENING: **Paolo Conte;** *Paolo Conte*

PROSCIUTTO E MELONE

{ ham and melon }

Without doubt the most famous Italian Twin, used sometimes as a summer second course that you can prepare quickly. It is also good for a picnic or vacation. Use only prosciutto (cured, uncooked Italian ham—San Daniele or Parma) sliced very thin. The cantaloupe has to be chosen with expertise. Smell both ends for aroma and feel for firmness (ends should give a little). After some experience, you will understand when the color is perfect.

Arrange sliced ham and pieces of melon in a pleasant way on a serving dish.

INGREDIENTS:
10 ounces of prosciutto   **2 cantaloupes**
SUGGESTED WINES: **Galestro**
RECOMMENDED LISTENING: **Beppe Gambetta;** *Dialogs*

❧ *Twins* ❧

UOVA DI QUAGLIA E CAVIALE

{ quail eggs and caviar }

This is not a typical Italian food, but who cares—it is a really high-class exotic.

Slice the hard-boiled eggs and serve with chilled caviar.

> **INGREDIENTS:**
>
> **8 quail eggs**
> **5 ounces of caviar**
>
> **SUGGESTED WINES:**
> **Champagne, Italian champenoise,**
>   *or* **Prosecco**
>
> **RECOMMENDED LISTENING:**
> **Vivaldi, Tartini, Mercadante, Boccherini;**
>   *Flute Concertos*, **Severino Gazzelloni**

FAVE E FORMAGGIO

{ fava beans and cheese }

A spring meal that doesn't need any serious preparation and comes from the tradition of the Lazio and Liguria regions.

Serve shelled fava beans and spicy cheese or have every guest shell the fresh fava beans and eat one of them with a little morsel of cheese.

> **INGREDIENTS:**
>
> **5 pounds of fresh fava beans**
> **1 pound of young fresh pecorino cheese**
>   *—if you cannot find pecorino, substitute with feta or similar type fresh sheep cheese*
>
> **SUGGESTED WINES:**
> **Zagarolo**
>
> **RECOMMENDED LISTENING:**
> **Nat King Cole;** *The Billy May Sessions*

PERE E FORMAGGIO

{ pears and cheese }

Another of the most delicious autumn dishes that you can prepare. Use imported Parmigiano-Reggiano cheese.

Slice the pears in quarters and put them in water with lemon juice to keep them white. Drain the pears to the last drop and dry them before arranging them on a serving dish with small chunks of Parmesan.

INGREDIENTS:

2 pounds of pears
½ pound of Parmigiano-Reggiano

SUGGESTED WINES:
Orvieto

RECOMMENDED LISTENING:
Delmore Brothers; *Brown's Ferry Blues*

DATTERI E MASCARPONE

{ dates and mascarpone }

We eat this sweet course in the winter, often at Christmas time. Because of the power of calories it is like a bomb, but if you eat it at the end of a lunch or dinner it's delicious! If you wish to take this recipe even a little further, serve the dates on a dish first covered with honey.

Take out the stones from dates and stuff them with mascarpone.

INGREDIENTS:

1 pound of dates
½ pound of mascarpone cheese

SUGGESTED WINES:
Moscato d'Asti, Vin Santo, Marsala,
Moscato Passito

RECOMMENDED LISTENING:
Paul O'Dette; Lute,
Robin is to the Greenwood Gone

My musician friend Luigi Grechi wrote this nice pesto epigram:

PREGHIERINA GENOVESE	GENOAN PRAYER
Signore, benedici questo pasto	*Oh Lord, bless this "pasto"(meal)*
Questo pesto	*This pesto*
E questo posto	*And this "posto"(place)*

PASTA COL PESTO

This delicious dish originated in Genoa and in the Ligurian region from where I come. Pesto is so well known and has so much importance in our culture that sometimes people give more evidence to the invention of pesto and linguine pasta than to the birth of "national heroes" like Nicoló Paganini or Christopher Columbus.

The following recipe is the Gambetta family version I learned from my grandmother and aunt Maria. In my family, on the subject of music, there were often arguments between my father, a big Verdi fan; my uncle Prospero, a Puccini fan; and grandpa Giuseppe, definitely on Donizetti's side. But on the subject of pesto, this is the recipe everyone agreed on.

The key to success with pesto is to use very fresh basil and the best olive oil and Parmesan you can find. Remove leaves of basil from stems and wash in water. Basil with large leaves may have an unwanted hint of mint. To adjust closer to the optimal flavor, blanch these leaves in boiling water for 37 seconds.

Ninety percent of the pesto produced in the world is done with a food processor, but the really good pesto is done by hand with a mortar and wooden pestle. There is a difference between the "destruction" of the basil leaves created by the blades of the mixer and the "squeezing" of the good juices that you obtain with a pestle.

If you use a mortar and pestle, the correct order of the ingredients is salt, garlic, pinenuts, basil and cheese. Add the oil at the very end and mix with a spoon until you reach a creamy consistency. If you use a food processor, the order of ingredients is not important. However, you should choose the low speed and stop the processor from time to time.

Always keep some leftover ingredients to add, if necessary, after dipping your little finger in the sauce and tasting with closed eyes. The oil and pinenuts give the bottom to the taste and the garlic, basil and cheese should be more in front but in good harmony.

Cook the pasta together with some peeled, sliced potatoes and string beans cut in half (added to the boiling water a few minutes before the pasta). Blend the pesto with drained pasta, potato and string beans. Sprinkle with grated Parmesan and serve immediately.

INGREDIENTS: *serves* **4**

- **16 ounces of pasta—linguine, lasagne, lasagne ricce** *or* **gnocchi**
- **4** *to* **6 supermarket bunches of fresh basil**
- **1** *or* **2 cloves of garlic**—*depending on your relationship with garlic*
- **salt to taste**
- **extra virgin olive oil**
- **½ cup of grated Parmesan**
- **½ cup of grated romano**
- **½ cup of pinenuts**—*depending on price*
- **two handfuls of string beans**
- **3 medium white potatoes**

OPTIONAL FOR VARIATION:
- **walnuts**
- **butter**
- **ricotta cheese**

TIME: **1 hour with mortar and pestle,** *or* **40 minutes with food processor**

DIFFICULTY: **Easy with attention and concentration**

SUGGESTED WINES:
Grignolino, Pigato, Dolcetto

RECOMMENDED LISTENING:
Nicolò Paganini; *Violin Concerto No.1, Sonata Napoleone,* **Salvatore Accardo**
Beppe Gambetta; *Good News From Home*
Enrique Coria; *The Guitar Artistry of Enrique Coria*

BRUSCHETTA

This is the perfect appetizer or snack that will lead you to any good meal. Sometimes, it can also be used as a side dish.

First I would like to teach you the perfect pronunciation of this difficult name—"bruce-ket´-ta." Say it this way and you will appear a connoisseur, surprising every Italian waiter or friend, and they will treat you with special regard. (Imagine how you could be surprised by an Italian saying phrases like "gimme a chicken-fried steak and side o' fries" with a perfect southern accent.)

This recipe is the right one to improvise the amounts of the ingredients as I told you in the introduction, so, let's try it!

Slice the tomatoes in small square pieces, put them in a bowl and take away a little part of the liquid if it seems too much. Add oil, salt, chopped parsley leaves, cayenne and black pepper until you like the taste very much. Stir and let it rest some minutes.

In the oven, toast the slices of bread until the surface becomes crisp and begins to change color. Rub the whole surface of every slice with a peeled garlic clove while the bread is still warm. The temperature will help the garlic to melt well into the bread.

Put the bread on a dish and cover the slices with the tomato mix (take it with a spoon so you will bring also some liquid). Try to eat it when it is still a little warm. For security reasons convince your partner to eat the same amount of bruschetta as you.

Many variations can be made of this salsa. Use basil instead of parsley or add a handful of tiny capers.

INGREDIENTS: *serves* **4–6**

1 pound of fresh tomatoes
fresh garlic
fresh parsley
olive oil
salt
black pepper—*fresh ground*
cayenne pepper
1 pound of medium thick sliced "Italian style" bread—*a sliced baguette works perfectly, but if you have access to a real Italian bakery ask for* **"Toscany style"** *bread or* **ciabatta**.

TIME: **20 minutes**

DIFFICULTY: **Easy**

SUGGESTED WINES:
Verduzzo, Prosecco, Trebbiano d'Aprilia

RECOMMENDED LISTENING:
Rossini; *Overtures*
Nuova Compagnia di Canto Popolare;
  Li Sarracini Adorano lu Sole
Doc Watson; *On Stage*

PEPERONI ARROSTITI

{ roasted peppers }

This preparation has the best relationship between quality and price that I know. Plus, it never comes bad. Of the recipes in this book, try this one first and you will surprise yourself and your guests with a spectacular dish.

The appearance of this dish will be very nice if you choose all the colors of peppers—red, yellow, orange and green. Also, the taste changes from pepper to pepper and the combination of all is the better choice.

Wash peppers in water. Roast them in a very hot oven or over the live fire and turn them frequently until the skins are blackened on all sides. Throw them in a paper bag and close the top. Let the peppers self-steam for at least 15 minutes. Take them out and peel them. Core them and remove their seeds. Slice in little "fillets." Put them on a plate and dress with the oil, salt and minced garlic. Before serving, turn peppers in the oil and garlic several times to allow them to absorb the flavors. Serve and enjoy the choir of "mmmmmmmmmh" of your guests.

INGREDIENTS: *serves* **4–6**

6 peppers
a pinch of salt
olive oil
fresh garlic

TIME: **50 minutes**

DIFFICULTY: **Easy**

SUGGESTED WINES:
Cortese di Gavi, Corvo Bianco, Vermentino

RECOMMENDED LISTENING:
Enrico Caruso; *Airs d'Operas et Melodies Milano 1902–1904*
Marino de Rosas; *Kiterras*
Steve Riley and the Mamou Playboys;
  Tit Galop Pour Mamou

CARBONARA

The "food and humor" columnist Calvin Trillin once started a campaign to change the national Thanksgiving dish from turkey to Spaghetti alla Carbonara. I'm quite sure this was a joke, but some truth was hidden in that proposal because the basic ingredients in Carbonara are really close to the traditional American breakfast. To describe Carbonara in a quick, understandable way, you could call it "pasta with bacon and eggs."

This southern Italian dish is fast and easy, but you need to pay careful attention to the timing. Because the eggs lose flavor and proper consistency when they cool down, it must be prepared and eaten immediately. No food schmoozing is allowed with Carbonara.

Sometimes, people in the north of Italy add whipping cream to Carbonara, but this is considered heresy or more simply a trick to reach the creamy consistency in an improper way (however, the trick does work well). About the topic of cheating with cream, a friend of mine told me one day a highly philosophical reflection: "Cooks are hiding their mistakes under whipped cream or mayonnaise. Doctors are hiding their mistakes in the ground under some meters of earth. Lawyers are hiding their mistakes behind prison bars. Guitar players are hiding their mistakes behind the distortion device and, in Bluegrass music, behind the noise of the banjo."

Beat the eggs in a large bowl and add a little bit of pepper and the cheese. Slice bacon in small cubes. Brown the cubed bacon with a few spoons of oil and the butter. (For more strong taste some people add to the browning bacon a smashed clove of garlic, which is removed at the end.) Adjust with salt and pepper and then take it off the fire. Let it cool a little and then mix with the eggs and cheese.

Meanwhile, cook the spaghetti. Drain it and throw it really quickly in a bowl with the sauce and stir it really fast. This will allow the heat of the pasta to lightly cook the eggs and give the perfect, creamy consistency. As a variation, some chefs sprinkle finely chopped parsley on this dish before serving.

INGREDIENTS: *serves* **4**

1 pound of spaghetti
3½ ounces of pancetta *or quality* **American bacon**
½ ounce of butter
2 ounces of grated pecorino romano
4 eggs
olive oil
salt
pepper

TIME: **25 minutes**

DIFFICULTY: **Easy**

SUGGESTED WINES:
Riviera del Garda Rosso, Chianti, Grignolino

RECOMMENDED LISTENING:
Italian String Virtuosi; *Italian String Virtuosi*
Pino Daniele; *Live Sció*
Leo Kottke; *6 & 12 String Guitar*

FOCACCIA AL FORMAGGIO

{ cheese bun }

This dish is a sort of pie that you can find (made in the right way) only in the towns of Recco and Camogli, near Genoa. This course is really the most traditional plate of my infancy and through all my life because I used to spend my holidays in that area in an ancient, little, picturesque house of my old relatives on the seaside. Now every time I have foreign guests, I drive them there and let them taste this delicious course. In my opinion the better way to have this focaccia experience is to buy it in a bakery towards the evening and eat it from the paper while walking in front of the shore and listening to the music of the sea.

Cut the cheese in thin slices, put it in a bowl and submerge in milk. After it has soaked for some time, crush it and blend with the milk to the consistency of yogurt.

Put some warm water and a few tablespoons of oil into a bowl and emulsify with a fork. On a pastry board make a little "mountain" of flour and dig into the top to form a little "volcano." Sprinkle some pinches of salt over the flour. Pour a little of the water and oil mixture into the "crater" and using your hands slowly and carefully incorporate more and more liquid into the flour until you are able to form a ball of dough. Knead the dough and as necessary add flour or water until it reaches an "elastic" consistency. Remember to cook by eye and sense. My grandma says the best way to check the consistency is to compare it with the ear lobe. Divide the dough in half and let it rest under a towel for a few moments.

Sprinkle some flour on the pastry board, the rolling pin and your hands and roll out two very thin layers of pasta. If you are brave enough to try it, this procedure comes best if you don't use a rolling pin but carefully stretch the pasta by hand.

With one layer, line an oiled metal baking sheet. Spread a thick and even amount of the softened cheese over the layer of pasta. Cover this with the second layer of pasta and close tight (pressing with fingers) the border.

INGREDIENTS: serves **4**

2¾ cups of flour
water and olive oil—*by sense and eye*
salt
14 ounces of stracchino cheese *or if you cannot find it use* ½ **feta** *and* ½ **ricotta**
milk

TIME: **45 minutes**

DIFFICULTY: **Easy**
(is more difficult to explain than to do it!)

SUGGESTED WINES:
Vermentino, Erbaluce di Caluso, Pinot Bianco. *Some happy, dry white wine like* **Vermentino** *is, in my opinion, the better choice to marry with the taste of focaccia al formaggio. The common rules don't suggest to drink beer with Italian food but rules are born to be changed, and among all the dishes presented in this book, this is most appropriate to experiment with a good beer.*

RECOMMENDED LISTENING:
Corelli; *Concerti Grossi Op. 6,*
    Ensemble 415
Fabrizio De Andrè; *Creuza De Mä*
Marco Pereira; *Dança dos quatro ventos*

Spread the surface of the bun with a thinner layer of cheese and a drizzle of oil. Place in the oven at 450–500 degrees. Watching carefully, let it bake until the surface turns a soft, yellow color with a few browned spots. Serve very warm.

Along with Carbonara, this is probably the most famous international Italian pasta dish. Many of you have probably already eaten it, but you will be surprised how much better a really good, fresh, homemade Amatriciana is than any average restaurant Amatriciana.

This recipe comes from central Italy from the little village of Amatrice in the mountains of Lazio region. The traditional pasta used for this dish is "bucatini" (empty spaghetti, sometimes difficult to find but paradise for children who like to whistle in them while eating to create "sauce medals" on the clothes of the whole family). Penne or similar pasta could also be good with this sauce.

You can make a difference in the taste of this sauce by using Italian pancetta or, better, guanciale (a special bacon that comes from the chop of the pork). The nuance will also change if the pancetta is smoked with pepper or with salt. Another improvement in the quality will be made by using fresh, peeled tomatoes and tasty, fresh grated pecorino romano.

Generally, Italian dishes are seldom strongly spicy. Medium spicy, if required, is the most common situation because if the spices are too strong, they take away from the rest of the taste. Amatriciana is one dish that "accepts" a particularly strong spicy taste without losing the other tastes. So, if you like, you can be really generous with the hot cayenne pepper.

Cut the bacon in small cubes. In a pan, cook the cubed bacon with a few spoons of oil then remove it from the grease and set aside. Brown the sliced onion in the grease (add a little more oil if necessary), add salt and pepper and cook until tender. Add the tomatoes, peeled and cut into small pieces, to the pan with the onions. Add also the bacon and cook moderately for 20 minutes. Stir from time to time and adjust the taste as you like with the red pepper and sing or whistle "O sole mio."

In the meantime, prepare the pasta pan and cook the bucatini. Drain the bucatini and season with the sauce, adding a little of the grated pecorino. Serve with grated pecorino to be sprinkled on top.

INGREDIENTS: *serves* **4**

- **1 pound of pasta—bucatini** *or* **penne**
- **4 ounces of guanciale magro**—*if you don't find* **guanciale** *you can use* **Italian pancetta** *or the* **best bacon** *you can find*
- **½ pound of fresh ripe tomatoes**
- **1 small onion cut in thin round slices**
- **cayenne pepper**
- **salt**
- **pepper**
- **2 tablespoons of extra virgin olive oil**
- **2 ounces of pecorino romano**

TIME: ½ hour

DIFFICULTY: Easy

SUGGESTED WINES:
Freisa, Barbera, Bonarda

RECOMMENDED LISTENING:
Nino Rota; *La Strada, Ballet Suite,* **Ricardo Muti**
R. Tesi, P. Vaillant, J.M. Carlotti, D. Craighead; *Anita Anita*
Dan Crary; *Jammed If I Do*

PASTA E ZUCCHINI

This is a particularly easy recipe that comes perfect when the zucchini are sliced to the size of a matchstick. To make this crucial cut, I always travel with my zucchini slicer in my baggage (together with my inseparable mini espresso machine), and to tell you the truth, this is really worth it. I have discovered that you can find these slicers in the United States in the better cooking stores. Look for a julienne slicer that produces this fine cut.

Cut the zucchini like little matchsticks and sauté them in a frying pan with olive oil. Drink some sips of wine with your friends until the zucchini begins to change color and consistency. Then add minced garlic and crumbled bouillon cube and cook for a short time. Here I will tell you a little secret about how to sauté garlic. In this recipe try to keep the garlic on top of the zucchini and off the bottom of the pan. If the garlic cooks too much it will become bitter and lose its fresh taste.

Cook and drain the pasta, flavor with this mixture and serve with grated Parmesan and a pinch of pepper.

INGREDIENTS: *serves* **4**

16 ounces of pasta—farfalle *or* **other short pasta**
1 pound of zucchini
3 tablespoons of extra virgin olive oil
1 bouillon cube of your choice
salt
pepper
grated Parmesan

TIME: **½ hour**

DIFFICULTY: **Easy**

SUGGESTED WINES:
Regaleali Bianco, Cinqueterre di Riomaggiore, Frascati

RECOMMENDED LISTENING:
Geminiani; *Concerti Grossi,* **I Musici**
La Ciapa Rusa; *Antologia*
Oregon; *Always, Never and Forever*

SUGO CRUDO

{ pasta with uncooked ingredients }

This is a typical summer dish and is prepared with all uncooked, sliced ingredients, but you cannot call it pasta salad because usually it is eaten when pasta is still warm. The temperature is important because the warm pasta brings the taste together and melts the cheese in the right way.

You can call this dish "the pasta of good health" because the raw ingredients are all friendly to the health for different reasons. There could be some concern about the animal fat in the cheese, but none is perfect.

Some companies produce pastas with a special consistency for this summer dish, for example, "Fresche Fantasie" by Barilla. If you can't find it, use a short pasta like farfalle, rotelle, etc.

There are many variations of ingredients for Sugo Crudo but this is my personal choice.

Chop the ingredients and mix them in a big bowl. Cook the pasta and drain it. Let the pasta cool in the colander for one minute so it will not melt the cheese too much. Add pasta to the bowl of chopped ingredients and mix it quickly. Taste for desired flavor and adjust with cheese, cayenne and oil. Put the Giuseppe Verdi CD on track 15 (va, pensiero) and serve with pride.

NOTE ABOUT MOZZARELLA:

Mozzarella is the most imitated cheese in the world. To confuse you, you find in supermarkets large packages of strange, yellowish cheese crumbs or cheese bars with the name mozzarella on it. Mozzarella is a white, fresh cheese with the shape of a ball that swims in its own water. It is produced from buffalo milk, Mozzarella di Bufala, or cow milk, Mozzarella Fior di Latte. The main regions of production are in the south of Italy but some Italian cheese artisans have exported this art to many fortunate places around the globe. The big defect of real mozzarella is that it is so good that often the entire production is eaten by the cheesemaker and his friends. I understand this really well because the only time in my life I arrived late for a gig was in Abruzzi region after being seduced by the mozzarellas of a tiny, mountain factory.

INGREDIENTS: *serves* **4**

- **16 ounces of pasta**
- **½ pound of fresh ripe tomatoes**
- **2 supermarket bunches of basil**
- **2 cloves of garlic**
- **cayenne pepper**
- **2 balls of fresh mozzarella**
- **5 tablespoons of extra virgin olive oil**
- **grated pecorino romano**

TIME: **½ hour**

DIFFICULTY: **Very, very easy**

SUGGESTED WINES:
Greco di Tufo, Locorotondo, Ravello

RECOMMENDED LISTENING:
Giuseppe Verdi; *Nabucco (highlights)*, **Domingo-Sinopoli**
Riccardo Tesi; *Un Ballo Liscio*
Sabicas; *Flamenco Puro*

SUGO CRUDO

— variation —

If you like the taste of uncooked sauce, you have to taste this one that I learned only recently from an ethnic music radio announcer in Rome. When he shared the recipe, we were sitting in a bar drinking cappuccino. Paolo was telling me the recipe with such a strong passion that a man who was sitting at the next table came to us and asked permission to copy the recipe because he was so impressed by this passionate explanation.

Cut zucchini in matchstick size pieces. Peel the tomatoes (after throwing them in boiling water for few seconds to help you in the work) and cut them in very little squares. Briefly sauté a few whole cloves of garlic in olive oil. After browned, remove the garlic and set the oil aside.

Mix in a big bowl the zucchini, tomatoes, broken tuna fish, olives without stones, washed and dried capers, chopped basil and oregano and add a little minced, uncooked garlic.

Cook the pasta, drain and throw it in the bowl of uncooked ingredients, mix it quickly and at the very end add the garlic-flavored oil. Add some cayenne pepper to taste. No cheese is necessary for this recipe.

(This is a good recipe for people on non-dairy diet.)

INGREDIENTS: *serves* **4**

16 ounces of short pasta
½ pound of fresh tomatoes
a tablespoon of capers in oil or salt
a handful of green and black olives
1 small can of tuna fish
1 *or* **2 little zucchini**
fresh oregano to taste
6 tablespoons of olive oil
garlic to taste
cayenne pepper to taste

TIME: **½ hour**

DIFFICULTY: **Easy**

SUGGESTED WINES:
**Trebbiano d'Abruzzo, Lugana, Bianco di
    Pitigliano**

RECOMMENDED LISTENING:
Vivaldi; *Mandolin Concertos,*
    I Solisti Veneti
Elena Ledda e Sonos; *Incanti*
Modern Mandolin Quartet; *Pan American
    Journeys*

Pasta e Broccoli is a southern Italian recipe and until a few years ago it was typically a winter season plate. Now it is possible to make this dish the whole year long because of technology. However, sometimes broccoli grown out of season doesn't match the standard that this recipe requires.

The concept of this food is the simple marriage between broccoli, sautéed garlic and pasta. If you have fresh broccoli in your garden, you can also try the recipe without adding the anchovies or capers. They are essential, however, to give some more "life" to the taste of broccoli out of season.

Wash the broccoli and cut it into flowerets. In a pasta pan of boiling water cook the broccoli alone and after 10 minutes add the orecchiette and cook together in the same water. Drain after pasta is "al dente."

When pasta is close to being ready, put the oil in a skillet and add finely chopped garlic and anchovies while the oil is cold. Remove from heat as soon as the garlic and anchovies start to fry. Throw the drained pasta and broccoli into the skillet, mix it well then add the cheese and "buon appetito."

A tasty variation can be done by adding cayenne pepper to taste and a handful of capers (washed of the salt) to the garlic and anchovies in the skillet.

Some cooks do the preparation with the broccoli and pasta cooked separately, but I'm sure the way I told you is the best because I learned it from Nanni Monetti, great cook at the restaurant "Quel che c'é c'é" ("What you will find you will find") in Arezzo Cincelli. As far as I know, Nanni is the only Italian banjo player and cook, so we must follow the pursuit of this multitalented artist.

INGREDIENTS: *serves* **4**

10 ounces of broccoli
14 ounces of pasta—orecchiette *(if you don't find orecchiette use other short pasta)*
5 tablespoons of extra virgin olive oil
2 cloves of garlic
2 salted anchovies *or* **equivalent of anchovy paste**
½ cup of grated Parmesan *or* **pecorino** *(depending if you like soft or strong taste)*

OPTIONAL FOR VARIATION:
cayenne pepper
two spoons of capers

TIME: **45 minutes**

DIFFICULTY: **Rather easy**

SUGGESTED WINES:
Lugana, Eloro Rosso, Corvo Bianco

RECOMMENDED LISTENING:
Puccini; *La Boheme (highlights)*, **Freni-Pavarotti-Panerai**
Roberto Murolo; *Roberto Murolo*
Bela Fleck; *Drive*

MINESTRONE

I got this recipe from Mafalda, my sister's mother-in-law. "Once happened at night…" I was with my family and we enjoy to see each other because it can happen only a few times in the year so when we can assemble it is a big joy. We were speaking about food and I was telling them about my "Gypsy" Minestrone, a sort of soup that I prepared in a country house with friends using a very big pot and cooking on the wooden fire, when someone asked me: "What are the ingredients you used?" "The ones that I found, of course. With friends and happiness all is good and the smoke from the open air fire gave the bottom to the flavor that made the difference." "Yes, but the soup of Mafalda is insuperable and changes with the seasons." That made me curious—really I became curious very quickly—and so I phoned Mafalda to ask her. She was proud to let us know how she does it and so here you have the instructions for two different seasons and strength of flavor.

In this description of the preparation of Minestrone I mention both summer and winter ingredients. I will trust you to choose the seasonal and additional ingredients available to you at the time of cooking.

In a big pot of water put the pork rind, pancetta, and a piece of Parmesan rind and begin to cook. Wash the vegetables, cut them into cubes and add to the pot. Also add one whole peeled potato. Hold the peas and cabbage to add later.

After 2 hours of cooking take out the big potato, break it up with a fork and return it to the pot. This helps give the soup its good consistency. Add peas and leaves of cabbage, cut in thin slices. When the soup boils again, add the rice or pasta. After about 10 minutes add the minced parsley, garlic and basil or pesto and let it finish cooking.

Serve with grated Parmesan, pepper and olive oil. In Piedmont they put one half glass of red wine in the serving plate before spooning in the Minestrone. You might try this in a small amount before serving it this way because you may or may not like it.

❖ *Summer* ❖

INGREDIENTS:	serves **4–6**

10 ounces of pinto (lumé) beans
4 ounces of French filets *or* **other string beans**
1 average size eggplant (melanzana)
5 zucchini
2 potatoes
2 peeled fresh tomatoes
1 large peeled potato
4 tablespoons of olive oil
2 quarts of water
9 ounces of rice *or* **short pasta— ditali rigati, bricchetti,** *etc.*

TIME: *The more it cooks the better—you need about* **20 minutes to prepare it,** **2½ hours or longer to cook it** *and a few minutes to eat it.*

DIFFICULTY: **Easy with patience**

This kind of soup is excellent during every part of the year. Serve it warm in winter and cold in summer. To taste it in the best way, you will have to put it in the plates one half hour before eating.

*Beppe serving Minestrone
to Zia Maria (on left)
and Mamma Gambetta.*

HANS-BERND SICK

MINESTRONE

❧ *Winter* ❧

INGREDIENTS: *serves* **4–6**

6 green leaves of cabbage *or* leaves of beets
4 handfuls of dried chick peas (canellini beans)
9 ounces of pumpkin *or* carrots
4 *or* 5 potatoes
several stalks of celery
1 large peeled potato
2 quarts of water
9 ounces of rice *or* short pasta— ditali rigati, bricchetti, *etc.*

❧ *Summer & Winter Variations* ❧

OPTIONAL FOR VARIATION:
In accordance with how powerful you like the flavor of the dish you can add these ingredients to both the "Summer" and "Winter" recipes:
1 onion
1 leek *(in spring)*
2 ounces of pancetta (Italian bacon)
4 ounces of pork rind
a piece of Parmesan rind
1 full spoon of tomato paste
1 can of peas
parsley
basil
garlic
A typical Genoese habit is to add at the very end some spoons of strong pesto.

SUGGESTED WINES:
Riesling di Colli Berici, Barbera d' Asti, Freisa

RECOMMENDED LISTENING:
Respighi; *Pines of Rome, Fountains of Rome*
Ivano Fossati; *Buontempo, Vol. 1*
Gene Parsons; *Melodies*

TOMAXELLE

Now I would like to introduce a very tasty but difficult recipe. The name of this plate is derived from the Latin "tomachulum"—a sort of short fat salami. Tomaxelle is an ancient recipe and was prepared the first time for a group of Austrian officers imprisoned in Genoa during the siege in eighteenth century.

Wash the porcini mushrooms and put them in a little bowl of warm water to become soft again. Also, soak the piece of bread in some warm milk. Peel and chop the tomatoes.

In a bowl put the minced veal, eggs, minced marjoram, minced mushrooms, the Parmesan, the bread (squeezed of the milk), minced parsley and garlic, the pinenuts and the salt. Okay, now you have to mix all very well. This is the stuffing for the veal rolls.

Using a meat pounder, flatten out the slices of veal and cover the surface of each piece with a little of the stuffing. Roll up the veal and tie it with a sewing thread. These rolls are the "tomaxelle."

Sprinkle the tomaxelle with flour and brown them in a skillet with butter. Add the salt, pepper and wine. When the wine has evaporated, add the tomatoes, the peas and cook for about 30 minutes. Turn the tomaxelle a few times while cooking and add some warm water if the sauce becomes too dry. If you wish be a polite host, remove the ties of thread before serving.

INGREDIENTS: serves **4**

4 slices of veal—fesa (upper part of leg)
½ pound of minced veal
2 eggs
7 ounces of little shelled peas—*fresh, if possible*
1 ounce of dried porcini mushrooms
1 full spoon of grated Parmesan
the soft part of one piece of bread
1 sprig of fresh marjoram—*this taste is really important in this dish, so add until distinct*
1 clove of garlic
1 tuft of parsley
2 tablespoons of pinenuts (Mediterranean pinoli)
2 ounces of butter
10 ounces of tomatoes
1 glass of dry white wine
salt
pepper
flour

TIME: **about 1 hour**

DIFFICULTY: **Some long preparation**

SUGGESTED WINES:
Montecarlo Rosso, Dolcetto di Ovada, Marzemino

RECOMMENDED LISTENING:
***A Room with a View*, Soundtrack**
Various Artists; *Canti Randagi*
Gambetta/Trischka; *Alone and Together*

PASTA E FAGIOLI

This dish has a consistency of a soup but is much more than a common soup—it is the greatest soup. It is basically a northern dish (although you can find it also sometimes in southern regions) and is really perfect for the winter season. It is typically a "warm up" meal, but in the warm months you can let it cool down and eat it lukewarm. The whole "timing" philosophy for Pasta e Fagioli (and also Minestrone) is sort of opposite than the other pastas that need to be eaten immediately after they are ready. Pasta e Fagioli becomes better in taste some hours after it is cooked—even the day after, it's really good—and it doesn't need to be eaten really warm. The final taste of the dish will change a lot, depending to the amount of "dressing" ingredients that each guest will add.

I'm embarrassed to talk about it, but there is also a delicate consideration about a sort of danger for the community that this food brings in the air some hours later. To warn people in a polite way I will copy an expression from the Artusi manuscript—the "bible" of the old-style Italian cuisine. Artusi just tells that some food can be more or less "windy," so please be careful because Pasta e Fagioli can really create a gale.

Shell the fresh beans. (If you use dry beans put them in cold water 12 hours before, and at the moment of cooking you rinse the beans and use them like the fresh ones.) Peel and cube the potatoes. Peel the tomatoes and cut into pieces.

Put the potatoes and beans in a big pot to boil in four quarts of water. Add the tomatoes and salt to taste. One hour later, when all the ingredients are well cooked on a slow fire, take away two big ladles of beans and purée them using a hand mixer or food processor. Return the puréed beans to the soup and mix. Now add the pasta and boil all together. Be careful. If you cook it with too strong fire, it will attach to the floor of the pan. Stir it and control it!

Mince the garlic and parsley leaves. Sauté them briefly in a frying pan with the oil and add to the soup toward the very end of the cooking process.

Serve Pasta e Fagioli with grated Parmesan, olive oil, and freshly ground black pepper for every guest to add depending on his own taste. Some people also add vinegar. Try a little on the side of the plate; you might like it or hate it.

INGREDIENTS: *serves* **4–6**

- **2 pounds of fresh pinto beans** *or* **1 pound of dry beans**
- **2 large white potatoes**
- **2 ripe tomatoes**
- **2 cloves of garlic**
- **1 little bunch of parsley**
- **9 ounces of pasta—fresh pappardelle** (*sort of large fettuccine*), **bricchetti,** *or* **ditali rigati**
- **4 tablespoons of olive oil**
- **salt and pepper to taste**
- **½ cup of grated Parmesan**

TIME: **2 hours + time to soak dry beans**

DIFFICULTY: **Quite easy**

SUGGESTED WINES:
Sangiovese di Romagna, Bardolino Rosso, Teroldego

RECOMMENDED LISTENING:
Giuseppe Verdi; *Aida,* **Chiara-Pavarotti**
Lucio Dalla, Francesco De Gregori; *Banana Republic*
Joe Carr, Alan Munde; *Windy Days and Dusty Skies*

Artichokes have a big role in the Italian cooking culture. There are an incredible number of ways of cooking them—in casserole, in the oven or with pasta. People eat them also raw in the salad or by dipping single leaves in an oil-based sauce called "pinzimonio." There are different kinds of artichokes and unfortunately outside of Italy it is very difficult to find the most tasty kind of this vegetable with dark green and strong thorny leaves.

The secret to the success of risotto stays also in the choice of the rice. There are many good short-grain Italian rices but the one most available in the United States is Arborio. Be careful not to substitute with long-grain or brown rice or you will starve, hopeless, in front of a pot of hard risotto.

To make the broth, you can choose normally a bouillon to your taste, but any fresh vegetable or meat broth available could make the difference. So, it is good to plan risotto in connection with any leftover soup. This recipe is quite romantic so be sure to have flowers and candles on the table before serving.

Clean the artichokes, cut off the top half (leaving mostly the heart), take away the tough external leaves and cut the stem (leaving only 2 or 3 centimeters). Cut the artichokes in thin slices lengthwise. While working with artichokes, always keep them in a bowl of lemon juice and water to avoid their turning dark.

Sauté the artichoke slices and chopped onion in a pan with half of the butter. Add the wine, mix and let the wine evaporate. Add a ladle of broth and let cook for about 10 minutes. Add the rice, stir and let it take the flavor. Adjust with salt and pepper.

Constantly stirring, add the rest of the broth slowly and regularly in little quantities taking care that the consistency of the risotto will never be too liquid or soupy. It will take around 15–20 minutes, and when the rice is cooked add the remaining butter and the cheese. Mix all together off of the fire and let the pan stay with a lid for a couple of minutes to form a soft, creamy texture. Place the risotto in a dish and serve with grated Parmesan.

INGREDIENTS: *serves* **4**

1 pound of rice
3 ounces of butter
1 bunch of little green onions
2 ounces of Parmesan cheese
4 artichokes
1 glass of dry white wine
4 cups of broth—*approximately*
black pepper
1 lemon

TIME: **45 minutes**

DIFFICULTY: **Quite easy with patience**

SUGGESTED WINES:
Ciró Rosato, Bianco di Pitigliano, Tocai

RECOMMENDED LISTENING:
Boccherini; *Guitar Quintets*
Tenores di Bitti; *Intonos*
Dick Siegel; *Angels Aweigh*

BUTTERO'S CHICKEN

This recipe comes from Toscany, a region on the border with Liguria where some Italian cowboys work in open air in the country near the sea. These men are called "Butteri" and work hard with horses and cattle, so they have always a big appetite.

This dish is the most appetizing way to cook chicken that I know, and I suggest you taste it with a very tonic and full-bodied wine in a party with a lot of friends. This is definitely the recipe to enjoy while listening to some cowboy music.

Cut the washed chicken in pieces. In a casserole sauté minced onion, garlic and cayenne, then add the bacon first minced with the sage. Add the pieces of chicken and pinenuts and brown over a speedy fire and add salt to taste.

Pour in the wine and using a wooden spoon loosen any ingredients that have attached to the bottom of the pan. When the wine has evaporated, add the tomatoes cut in pieces. Lower the fire and let cook covered with a lid. Stir from time to time and, if it needs it, add a little water or broth.

When chicken has cooked, add a sprinkling of vinegar. When the vinegar has evaporated, serve.

INGREDIENTS:	*serves* **4**

1 chicken—around 3 pounds
1 piece of onion
1 clove of garlic
2 spoons of pinenuts
4 tablespoons of olive oil
cayenne pepper
1 ounce of pancetta *or quality* American bacon
1 little bunch of sage
1 glass of red wine
½ pound of peeled tomatoes
a sprinkling of vinegar
salt

TIME: **A little bit more than 1 hour**

DIFFICULTY: **Easy**

SUGGESTED WINES:
Fara, Cannonau, Marzemino

RECOMMENDED LISTENING:
Toscanini with the NBC Symphony Orch.;
  Recording from 1939–1952
Franco Morone; *Guitarea*
Riders in the Sky; *The Best of the West*

This is the typical "Genovese" fish soup. The name is Arabic and is one of the few Arabic terms commonly used in the dialect that Genoese sailors introduced to the language in ancient times when the trade with the east was the main business in town. Historically, the main characteristic of the soup is to accept many different kinds of fish, depending on what you find fresh at the market, what you fish yourself or what fish is more affordable. For this recipe it is better to use a wooden spoon and a piece of terra-cotta crockery.

Wash the mushrooms and put them in a bowl of warm water to soften. In a large casserole sauté the peeled and softly crushed cloves of garlic, minced onions, carrots and celery in olive oil. Add in the next ingredients (all minced)—pinenuts, capers, anchovies without bones and mushrooms. This addition will be perfect if you mix and work these ingredients in a mortar and pestle first. Add the wine and thicken the sauce with a spoon of flour that you have diluted in a little warm water. Add salt and pepper, tomato paste and some minced fresh parsley and let cook for about 15 minutes.

Add the octopus to the pot and after about 15 minutes add the fish, cut in pieces. Add water or fish broth to obtain desired consistency. Cook by a slow fire. Do not stir the soup too much with a spoon to prevent breaking the fragile fish. Instead, mix by shaking the casserole. Add the shrimp and mussels at the very end and cook until the mussels open and the shrimp become pink.

Place toasted slices of bread that you have rubbed with fresh garlic in each serving bowl. Ladle the fish soup over the bread and serve.

INGREDIENTS: *serves* **4–6**

- olive oil
- garlic
- 2 onions
- 2 carrots
- several stalks of celery
- handful of pinenuts
- 3 *or* 4 salted anchovies
- 2 *or* 3 tablespoons of capers
- 1 glass of dry white wine
- 2 *or* 3 spoons of tomato paste
- 2 ounces of dried porcini mushrooms
- 1 bunch of parsley
- 1 spoon of flour
- 3 pounds of at least three kinds of saltwater fish
- ½ pound of little octopus
- ½ pound of shrimp
- 1 dozen mussels
- salt and pepper
- 1 pound of sliced Italian bread

TIME: **2 hours**

DIFFICULTY: **Some long preparation**

SUGGESTED WINES:
Vernaccia di S. Gimignano, Verdicchio di Matelica, Vermentino, Lumassina

RECOMMENDED LISTENING:
Puccini; *Tosca (highlights)*, Freni-Domingo-Sinopoli
Fabrizio De Andrè; *Le Nuvole*
Deanta; *Ready for the Storm*

TIRAMISÙ

The name Tiramisù (accent on the last letter) means in Italian "pick me up" and it is really appropriate since the bottom of the taste comes from the espresso coffee. This cake is really well known also outside of Italy because it has four great characteristics that everyone loves—it is simple, good, cheap and fast.

Tiramisù was invented in the last decade and this new development proves that the Italian cuisine is still in evolution. Who knows what will come next?

The perfection is proportional to the quality of some ingredients. Particularly, the mascarpone and the espresso need to be chosen with accuracy.

Separate the white from the yolk of the eggs. Whip the whites of the eggs. In another bowl, beat the yolks with the sugar until they become frothy. In a big bowl mix carefully with a wooden spoon the whites, the yolks and the mascarpone. In a deep dish blend coffee and Marsala. If you are bad, add some extra sugar. Dip some ladyfingers in this mixture (quickly so they do not get soggy). Line the bottom of a medium size springform pan or pan with a removable bottom with a layer of the ladyfingers. Cover them with a layer of the egg and cheese mixture and sprinkle with cocoa until surface is totally covered. Go on in this way as long as you have ingredients. Finish with cocoa and let it rest in the refrigerator for at least a couple of hours.

Variations of Tiramisù are made by using different liquors and reducing the amount of coffee.

INGREDIENTS: *serves* **6–8**

3 eggs
1 cup of espresso coffee
1 cup of Marsala wine
¼ pound of sugar
cocoa powder
8 ounces of mascarpone
**10 ounces of savoiardi biscuits
    (ladyfingers)**

TIME: **20 minutes + 2 hours in the fridge**

DIFFICULTY: **Easy**

SUGGESTED WINES:
Moscato, Vin Santo, Malvasia

RECOMMENDED LISTENING:
Maria Callas; *La Voce*
Francesco De Gregori; *Rimmel*
Martin Hayes; *Under the Moon*

CASTAGNACCIO

The general concept of this book is to present simple food that everyone loves with easy-to-find ingredients but this last recipe is an exception. Castagnaccio has a particular taste that some people love but not everyone likes and also might give you a big problem in the search of the main ingredient—chestnut flour. I like this flat "cake" a lot because it is a really ethnic food that, like some music, has its roots in ancient times.

Not many years ago our mountain lands of the Liguria region (very dry, steep and barren) were able to give the inhabitants only poor and frugal food. The main production was based on the chestnut and its by-products. For long periods during the winter the only meal was this cake in its essential form—flour, water and salt. Many elderly people dislike this dish because it reminds them of hard times. However, the younger generations love it because to them it brings fond memories of youth, school days and first flirtations when they offered Castagnaccio to the beautiful girl who suddenly disappeared.

I have read the recipe for Castagnaccio in seven cookbooks and every time it was slightly different. The same thing happened when I asked people living in the mountain villages. Every five miles something changed. So, I decided to try all the variations myself, and after thirteen experiments I can assure you that this is the better combination of ingredients for Castagnaccio.

Soak the raisins in a bowl of water to soften. In a large bowl put the flour and add milk, sugar, salt and lemon zest. Mix together until you don't see any lumps. If you have time let this mixture rest a while. Coat the inside of a shallow baking sheet with oil or, if you have it, use parchment paper and less oil. Slowly pour the batter onto the sheet. The batter should be about 1 centimeter (a little less than ½ inch) thick. Decorate the surface with the raisins, pinenuts and fennel seeds as if you were planting seeds. Some ingredients will sink into the batter, but, no problem. Adjust the amounts of these ingredients to your pleasure. Spread two spoons of oil over the surface and place in the oven. Bake at 350° for about 35 minutes. The cake is ready when there are many cracks in the surface and the edges are browned. Sprinkle the cake with powdered sugar and serve warm out of the oven or at room temperature.

INGREDIENTS: *serves* **6–8**

9 ounces of chestnut flour
2 cups of milk
4 *or* **5 spoons of sugar**
a pinch of salt
zest of 1 lemon
2 ounces of pinenuts
1 spoon of fennel seeds
3 *or* **4 ounces of raisins**
several spoons of olive oil
powdered sugar

TIME: **59 minutes**

DIFFICULTY: **Easy**

SUGGESTED WINES:
**Vino Santo Rosso, Moscato d'Asti,
    Moscato Passito**

RECOMMENDED LISTENING:
Scarlatti Avison; *12 Concerti Grossi*
Patrick Vaillant, Riccardo Tesi; *Véranda*
G. Larsen, A. Marchand; *The Orange Tree*

⇒ *The Nap* ⇐

In my opinion the little rest at the end of the meal is a basic moment to make complete the whole eating process and it should be considered a real part of it and planned in the proper way.

The Oriental philosophy is generally opposed to siesta because of the bad mood that it can bring, but fortunately in other parts of the world like Italy, Mexico, Spain and many others, siesta is still an important moment of the day. Even in the hectic lifestyle of the recent years, the good habit of siesta wasn't totally lost. In my country, for example, many families still eat together at noon and the shops are closed until 3:30 PM to leave the people the possibility to enjoy the nap after the meal. Siesta has in Italy a lot of regional names (pisolino, pennichella, controra, etc.) and can be done with many variations. It depends a lot on the amount of food and the metabolism of every single person. Some people, especially when they sleep too long and deep, feel strong headaches and bad digestion, while other people can sleep happily for hours and feel great. Everyone should choose his siesta in his own way and choose timing related to his body and to the schedule of the day.

After a little survey among friends, I can tell that the usual way to do siesta is to sleep for less than one hour sitting comfortably in a couch or armchair with a little blanket or similar on the stomach. The medium siesta time I found is 43 minutes and this is also what official scientists usually say. If siesta is less than one hour, it won't disturb the good relationship between sleep and waking. Siesta can be also done more seriously in bed for longer time, and if you like to do it well,

you better organize your room with a venetian blind or something similar to reach the comfortable darkness that the nap requires. On the opposite side, siesta can be also a moment of total relaxation and rest even without falling asleep. This moment can be devoted to listen to soft music, to pet the cat on the lap or to do nothing. Probably the wrong moment to do siesta is when you eat or drink really, really too much. It is a situation that shouldn't happen, but when it does, a little walk in the countryside can be a better help than a siesta.

Also, the survey revealed that sometimes siesta is used to make love. In this case, instructions can be found in other books but for sure they say is better to go quickly after eating to bed. Evidence can be found in an Italian mountain folk song that goes:

Di qua di là del Piave ci sta un'osteria
Là c'è da bere e da mangiare ed un buon letto
*   per riposar.*
E dopo aver mangiato, mangiato e ben bevuto
Se vuoi venire, o bella mora, questa è l'ora di
*   fare l'amor!*

On both sides of Piave river, you can find a
   tavern.
There will be food and drinks and a good
   bed to rest.
And after you will be finished to eat, to eat
   and to drink well,
If you like to come, oh beauty with dark
   hair, this is the time to make love!

From the food point of view, in this case it is good to leave some food (sweets in particular) for after. Tiramisù could be an appropriate choice.

❧ *Beppe* ❧

Born in Genoa, Italy, Beppe began his career in a classical music orchestra for plectrum instruments. After gaining exposure to a wide variety of musical genres, he chose to focus his studies on the guitar playing styles of American traditional music. Since then he has developed a distinctive sound of his own, a multicultural tapestry of traditional and original acoustic music forms.

Beppe's talents have been enjoyed at concert halls, international festivals and workshops throughout Europe, the United States and Canada. His original compositions and arrangements reflect a colorful mosaic of musical influences—native Italian music, Celtic, central European and mediterranean dance tunes, classical fingerstyle and American flatpicking. His novel approach attests to the far-reaching impact of American traditional music.

During one of his earliest tours stateside, Beppe recorded *Dialogs*, a collection of duets with some of acoustic music's most notable players. He then released *Alone and Together*, a live recording of a 1991 tour with banjo innovator Tony Trischka. In 1995, Green Linnet Records released Beppe's *Good News From Home*. This recording includes songs sung in Italian dialects, original compositions and traditional pieces from countries on both sides of the Atlantic. Beppe produced his first instructional video, "New Directions in Flatpicking," in 1995 for Homespun Tapes.

Serving as artistic director for several European festivals and summer music camps, Beppe opened new doors for American traditional music in Europe in 1977, when he founded the Italian bluegrass group Red Wine. An expert on flatpicking techniques, he published the first Italian manual on the subject, and a collection of transcriptions of solos by Bluegrass music's foremost guitar pickers. Beppe also contributes as a columnist and feature writer to several leading music journals, including Italy's *Chitarre* and Germany's *Musikblatt*.

In 1989, Beppe Gambetta received the distinguished "Paolo Nuti" award, given by Folkitalia, which recognizes artists who have played an exceptional role in the diffusion of traditional music and culture in Italy.

Beppe tours much of the year as a solo artist and has performed with Dan Crary, Tony Trischka, Gene Parsons and others. He has experienced the joy of sharing the stage with his son Filippo Clarence and also performs serenades, mazurkas, opera arias, and other rediscovered Italian turn-of-the-century music with classical mandolinist Carlo Aonzo, of La Scala Orchestra in Milan. When Beppe is not entertaining audiences in cities around the globe, cooking in foreign kitchens, or packing his suitcase, he makes his home in Genoa.

❧ *Discography* ❧

recordings:

Good News From Home (Green Linnet 2117)

Dialogs (Alcazar 123)
with:
Danny Weiss, Norman Blake,
Alan Munde, Mike Marshall,
John Jorgenson, Dan Crary,
Raul Reynoso, Rob Griffin,
Charles Sawtelle, David Grier,
Joe Carr, Phil Rosenthal

Alone and Together (Alcazar 118)
Tony Trischka and Beppe Gambetta

Full Taste (Red Wine 001)
Red Wine

Beppe Gambetta (BG001)

featured on:

Jammed If I Do (Sugar Hill 3824)
Dan Crary

Windy Days and Dusty Skies (Flying Fish 70644)
Joe Carr and Alan Munde

video instruction:

New Directions in Flatpicking
(Homespun Tapes VD–GAM–GT01)

published works:

Dialogs *(transcription companion to recording)*
24 Solos for Flatpicking Guitar
Flatpicking Guitar Manual
Metodo di Chitarra Country–Rock

Beppe with Mary & Rick

DISCOGRAPHY FOR RECOMMENDED LISTENING:

Scarlatti Avison
12 Concerti Grossi
(Philips, 438 806-2)

Boccherini
Guitar Quintets
(Teldec, 4509 97975-2)

Maria Callas
La Voce
(Suite Laudis srl, CDS 1-5002)

Joe Carr, Alan Munde
Windy Days and Dusty Skies
(Flying Fish, FF 70644)

Enrico Caruso
*Airs d'Operas et Melodies
Milano 1902-1904*
(EMI, CDH 761-462)

Nat King Cole
The Billy May Sessions
(Capitol Jazz, CDP 07777895452)

Paolo Conte
Paolo Conte
(CGD, 2292 46044-2)

Corelli
Concerti Grossi Op. 6,
Ensemble 415
(Harmonia Mundi, HMC 901
406.07)

Enrique Coria
The Guitar Artistry of Enrique Coria
(Acoustic Disc, ACD-6)

Dan Crary
Jammed If I Do
(Sugar Hill, SH CD 3824)

Lucio Dalla, Francesco De Gregori
Banana Republic
(RCA, PD 74839)

Pino Daniele
Live Sció
(CGD, 4509 98381-2)

Fabrizio De Andrè
Creuza De Mä
(Ricordi, CDMRL 6308)

Fabrizio De Andrè
Le Nuvole
(Ricordi, CDMRL 6444)

Francesco De Gregori
Rimmel
(RCA, PD70742)

Deanta
Ready for the Storm
(Green Linnet, GLCD 1147)

Delmore Brothers
Brown's Ferry Blues
(County Records, CCS-CD-116)

Bela Fleck
Drive
(Rounder, CD 0255)

Ivano Fossati
Buontempo, Vol. 1
(Epic, EPC 473901 2)

Beppe Gambetta
Good News From Home
(Green Linnet, GLCD 2117)

Beppe Gambetta
Dialogs
(Alcazar, ALC 123)

Gambetta/Trischka
Alone and Together
(Alcazar 118)

Geminiani
Concerti Grossi, I Musici
(Philips Serie Duo, 438766-2)

Martin Hayes
Under the Moon
(Green Linnet, GLCD 1155)

Italian String Virtuosi
Italian String Virtuosi
(Rounder, CD 1095)

Leo Kottke
6 & 12 String Guitar
(Rhino, 71612)

La Ciapa Rusa
Antologia
(Robi Droli, RDC 015)

G. Larsen, A. Marchand
The Orange Tree
(Sugar Hill, SH CD 1136)

Modern Mandolin Quartet
Pan American Journeys
(BMG Windham Hill Records
01934 11135-2)

Franco Morone
Guitarea
(Acoustic Music Records Best.
Nr. 319.1046.2)

Roberto Murolo
Roberto Murolo
(BMG-Ricordi, ATBCD 302212 /302212)

Nuova Compagnia di Canto
Popolare
Li Sarracini Adorano lu Sole
(EMI 3C 064-18026)

Paul O'Dette
Lute
Robin is to the Greenwood Gone
(Elektra Nonesuch, 9 79123-2)

Oregon
Always, Never and Forever
(veraBra Records, vBr 2073 2)

Nicolò Paganini
*Violin Concerto No.1, Sonata
Napoleone*, Salvatore Accardo
(Deutsche Grammophon, 439 981-2)

Gene Parsons
Melodies
(Sierra Records, OXCD 6010)

Marco Pereira
Dança dos quatro ventos
(GHA, 126.031)

Puccini
La Boheme (highlights),
Freni-Pavarotti-Panerai
(DECCA, 421245-2)

Puccini
Tosca (highlights),
Freni-Domingo-Sinopoli
(Deutsche Grammophon, 437547-2)

Respighi
*Pines of Rome
Fountains of Rome*
(Song, SBK 48 267)

Riders in the Sky
The Best of the West
(Rounder, 11517)

Steve Riley and the Mamou
Playboys
Tit Galop Pour Mamou
(Rounder, CD 6048)

A Room with a View, Soundtrack
(DRG Records, DRGCDSBL 12588)

Marino de Rosas
Kiterras
(RBS, 1990)

Rossini
Overtures
(RCA Classics, 74321212882)

Nino Rota
La Strada, Ballet Suite, Ricardo Muti
(Sony, SK 66279)

Sabicas
Flamenco Puro
(Hispa Vox, 7 98992 2)

Dick Siegel
Angels Aweigh
(School Kids Records, SCHO 1519)

Elena Ledda e Sonos
Incanti
(Silex, Y225029)

Tenores Di Bitti
Intonos
(Robi Droli, NT 6727 27)

Riccardo Tesi
Un Ballo Liscio
(Silex, Y225056)

R. Tesi, P. Vaillant, J.M. Carlotti,
D. Craighead
Anita Anita
(Silex, Y225037)

Toscanini with the NBC Symphony
Orchestra
Recording from 1939-1952
(RCA, GD 60308)

Patrick Vaillant, Riccardo Tesi
Véranda
(Silex, Y225002)

Various Artists
Canti Randagi
(BMG Ariola, TCD MRL 6509)

Giuseppe Verdi
Aida, Chiara-Pavarotti
(DECCA, 433162-2)

Giuseppe Verdi
Nabucco (highlights),
Domingo-Sinopoli
(Digital Stereo, 435415-2)

Vivaldi
Mandolin Concertos,
I Solisti Veneti
(Erato, 2292-45946-2)

Vivaldi, Tartini, Mercadante,
Boccherini
Flute Concertos,
Severino Gazzelloni
(Philips, 420-875-2)

Doc Watson
On Stage
(Vanguard, VCD 9/10)

North American Management:
Stephanie P. Ledgin
TML Entertainment
P.O. Box 10598
New Brunswick, NJ
08906-0598

phone: (908) 699-0665
fax: (908) 699-0570
e-mail: ledgin@rci.rutgers.edu

European Management:
Hans-Bernd Sick
Mozartstrasse 20
D-88400 Biberach
Germany

phone: 0049-7351-75396